NEVER SELL A
——— ON A WET DAY

Written and illustrated by
Mal Peet and Elspeth Graham

Collins Educational
An imprint of HarperCollinsPublishers

Proverbs say one thing, but they mean something else.

You might hear someone say:
> *People who live in glass houses should not throw stones.*

That's a proverb, and it's not really about throwing stones and houses made of glass. It means something like:
> *You shouldn't go around criticizing other people for doing bad things if you do the same bad things yourself.*

Proverbs can be useful because they are often a quick way of saying something quite complicated.

Many proverbs work by putting a picture into your mind. You can get the picture quickly even when the meaning of the proverb is difficult to understand.

It's quite hard to work out the meaning of:
Don't throw out the baby with the bathwater.
But it's quite easy to picture it.

Weather proverbs

One swallow doesn't make a summer.

One woodcock doesn't make a winter.

To catch the wind in a net

Every cloud has a silver lining.

Red sky at night, shepherd's delight.   *Red sky in the morning, shepherd's warning.*

Lightning never strikes in the same place twice!

Well, almost never...

Many proverbs are very, very old. They go back to the days when most people had to find or catch or grow their own food. That's why there are so many proverbs to do with farming and raising animals.

Make hay while the sun shines.

Never sell a hen on a wet day.

Don't put all your eggs in one basket.

Animal proverbs and sayings

The peacock has fine feathers but foul feet.

Why keep a dog and bark yourself?

The smallest crows have the biggest beaks.

Food proverbs and sayings

Because food and drink have always been so important, lots of proverbs and sayings are about cooking and eating and drinking.

Enough ale will make a cat talk.

It's a poor cook who won't lick his own finger.

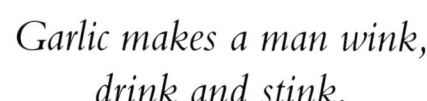

Garlic makes a man wink, drink and stink.

Proverbs at work

The barber learns to shave by shaving fools.

The doctor is more often to be feared than the disease.

The bad workman blames his tools.

As mad as a hatter.

Don't wash your dirty linen in public.

All work and no play makes Jack a dull boy.

Proverbs from other countries

All countries and languages have their own proverbs and sayings. Here are a few from other countries in Europe.

A dog does not stay tied to a sausage for long. (Germany)

When a bear is at your heels, don't look for his footprints. (Greece)

A guest and a fish stink after three days. (Italy)

Don't be deceived by the whiteness of the turban – you can get soap for nothing.
(Turkey)

Beware the woman with a beard and the man without one.
(Spain)

Never bolt the door with a boiled carrot. (Ireland)

Watery proverbs

To let the cat out of the bag means to cause trouble by giving away a secret. Most people think that is has something to do with a real cat hidden in a sack. It doesn't. The original meaning is much nastier. The 'cat' was the *cat o'nine tails*, a vicious leather whip with nine thin straps. It was used to punish sailors on the old sailing ships. To make the whip more supple, it was soaked in water inside a canvas bag. When the 'cat' was taken out of the bag, someone was in for trouble...

The birthday proverb

This well-known rhyming proverb seems a bit tough on children born on Wednesday.

Monday's child is fair of face,

Tuesday's child is full of grace,

Wednesday's child is full of woe,

Thursday's child has far to go,

Puzzle proverbs

Can you find proverbs in this book that fit the pictures on these pages?

Congratulations, Mrs Harvey! You've won a luxury skiing holiday!

She's a terrible gossip! Do you know what she told me the other day? She said that Chris went to the cinema with Rosie even though he said he'd go to the beach with Tessa! And I'll tell you something else about her...

Your homework is so messy, Sophie!

Please Miss, it's 'cos my pen writes all wobbly.

And it's not over… until the fat lady sings.